Raising a Bag of Toys:
Pulley vs. Inclined Plane

by Mari Schuh

first step nonfiction

Lerner Publications ◆ Minneapolis

LERNER

SOURCE

Expand learning beyond the printed book. Download free, complementary educational resources for this book from our website, www.lerneresource.com.

All images in this book are used with the permission of: © Todd Strand/Independent Picture Service except: © Michael Flippo/Dreamstime.com, p. 8 (bottom right); © Sergiy Kuzmin/Shutterstock.com, p. 8 (top left).

Front cover: © Todd Strand/Independent Picture Service.

Main body text set in ITC Avant Garde Gothic Std Medium 21/25.
Typeface provided by Adobe Systems.

Lerner Publications Company
A division of Lerner Publishing Group, Inc.
241 First Avenue North
Minneapolis, MN 55401 USA

For reading levels and more information, look up this title at www.lernerbooks.com.

Library of Congress Cataloging-in-Publication Data

Schuh, Mari C., 1975– author.
    Raising a bag of toys: pulley vs. inclined plane / by Mari Schuh.
        pages   cm. — (First step nonfiction. Simple machines to the rescue)
    Audience: Ages 5–8.
    Audience: K to grade 3.
    Includes index.
    ISBN 978-1-4677-8024-7 (lib. bdg. : alk. paper) — ISBN 978-1-4677-8298-2 (pbk.) —
ISBN 978-1-4677-8299-9 (EB pdf)
    1. Pulleys—Juvenile literature. 2. Simple machines—Juvenile literature. I. Title.
TJ1103.S38 2014
621.8—dc23   2014037379

Manufactured in the United States of America
4-43733-18732-2/14/2017

Table of Contents

Jake and Emma want to bring toys to Mia's fort.

What can help them?

An inclined plane has a slanted surface.

Jake wants to try an **inclined plane**.

A pulley is made of a wheel and a rope.

Emma wants to try a **pulley**.

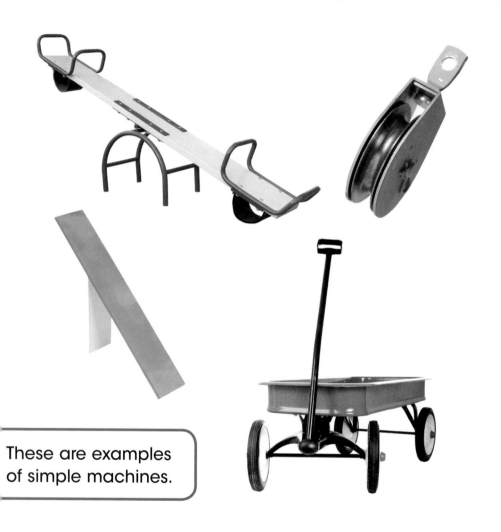

These are examples of simple machines.

Inclined planes and pulleys are **simple machines**.

Jake uses a slide. A slide is a type of inclined plane.

He pushes the toys up the slide.

Jake cannot reach the top.
The slide is too tall.

The bag of toys is heavy.
It falls.

Next, Emma uses a pulley.

A pulley has a wheel. A rope fits in a **groove**.

When the rope moves, the wheel turns. The wheel helps the rope move objects.

Emma attaches the bag.

Jake puts the toys in the bag.

A Pulley Saves the Day!

Emma pulls the rope. The wheel turns.

A pulley can lift objects.

The bag goes up.

Mia gets the toys!

A pulley can lower things too.

How can you use a pulley?

A pulley makes **work** easier!

Glossary

groove – a long, narrow cut in an object

inclined plane – a slanted surface

pulley – a wheel that helps a rope lift and lower objects

simple machines – machines with one moving part or no moving parts

work – moving an object by pushing or pulling

Index